Christmas Play

by
Gary Neal Hansen

The Story of the Coming of Jesus,
for Production in Churches, Using the Text of the
English Standard Version of the Bible

Climacus Publishing
Well grounded. Aiming high.

Spoken text: From the *ESV*® *Bible* (*The Holy Bible, English Standard Vesion*®), copyright 2001 by Crossway, a publishing ministry of Good News Publishers. Used by permission. All rights reserved.

Christmas Play: The Story of the Coming of Jesus, for Production in Churches, Using the Text of the English Standard Version of the Bible

© 2015, Gary Neal Hansen

All Rights Reserved

CAUTION: Professionals and amateurs are hereby warned that performance of CHRISTMAS PLAY is subject to a Licensing Fee. It is fully protected under the copyright laws of the United States of America and (to the best of the author's knowledge) of all countries with which the United States has copyright treaties or other reciprocal agreements. All rights, including professional and amateur stage rights, motion picture, recitation, lecturing, public reading, radio broadcasting, television, video or sound recording and all other forms of mechanical or electronic reproduction or storage and photocopying, and the rights of translation into foreign languages, are strictly reserved. Inquiries should be made through GaryNealHansen.com.

Live stage performance rights to CHRISTMAS PLAY are controlled exclusively through GaryNealHansen.com, and licenses must be secured in advance of performance. When requesting a performance license please indicate the number and dates of performances.

Please note that the Licensing Fee must be paid whether the play is presented for charity or gain and whether or not admission is charged. Likewise permission to photocopy scripts is prohibited except when licensed through GaryNealHansen.com

So…

For licensing of productions and permissions to reproduce scripts please go to GaryNealHansen.com/christmas-play.

Paperback ISBN: 978-0-9864124-2-4
EBook ISBN: 978-0-9864124-3-1

ACKNOWLEDGEMENTS

I give my sincere thanks to the following people, all of whom made this a better work:

Lesley Abrams, Tim Slemmons, and Dawna Duff for reading and commenting on drafts of this play.

Teddi Black for cover design and interior design.

The kind people at Crossway for generously granting permission to reproduce the ESV text in print and performance.

DEDICATION

For Michael Self, my first director,
with thanks for his wise final note to the cast before opening night:

"If all else fails, loud and fast."

.

Christmas Play

ALSO BY GARY NEAL HANSEN

Kneeling with Giants: Learning to Pray with History's Best Teachers

The Kneeling with Giants Reader: Writings on Prayer by History's Best Teachers

Small Group Leader's Guide to Kneeling with Giants

Love Your Bible: Finding Your Way to the Presence of God with a 12th Century Monk

Love Your Bible Small Group Leader's Guide

Sign up for Gary Neal Hansen's newsletter,
and get a free ebook.
Just go to GaryNealHansen.com/subscribe

Christmas Play

CHARACTERS

* Indicates characters seated on the row of chairs throughout.

NARRATOR
Stands at the pulpit or lectern.

*MARY
Young woman on whom the story hinges; she will become the mother of the Son of God, the savior of humanity.

*HEROD
Governor of Judea. Sits on his throne throughout, a reminder of the powers opposed to Christ. Should wear a crown.

*ZECHARIAH
Aged priest and husband of Elizabeth. He will become the father of John the Baptist. Great part for an older member of the congregation. (Played by the same actor as Simeon. Indicate the change by a costume element such as the presence or absence of Middle-Eastern headdress.)

*ELIZABETH
Cousin of Mary, and aged wife of Zechariah. She will become the mother of John the Baptist. Great part for an older member of the congregation. (Played by the same actor as Anna. Indicate the change with a costume element such as a head scarf.)

*GABRIEL
Archangel. Can be played by a male or female actor.

JOSEPH
Carpenter who is betrothed to Mary; he will become the stepfather of Jesus.

*LAW AND PROPHETS
An actor who personifies the voice of Scripture, called upon to read various Old Testament passages quoted as fulfilled in the coming of Jesus. Can be played by a male or female actor.

INNKEEPER
Citizen of Bethlehem working in the hospitality industry. Can be played by a male or female actor.

ANGELS
At least two angels are needed in addition to Gabriel to make up the heavenly host. The number can be expanded to fit the desired size of cast. Can be played by male or female actors.

SHEPHERDS
At least two shepherds are needed, but the number can be expanded to fit the desired size of cast. Can be played by male or female actors (shepherds in the Ancient world could be of either gender).

WISE MEN
The Bible does not say how many there were. People assume there were three because three gifts are mentioned (gold, frankincense, and myrrh). The Scriptural term is "magi," though it is most frequently translated "wise men." They could be of any age or gender to fit the needed size of cast.

*SIMEON
Aged citizen of Jerusalem; a pious man who had received God's promise that he would see the savior. A great role for an older member of the congregation. (Played by the same actor as Zechariah, with a small costume element, such as middle eastern headdress, to indicate the change.)

*ANNA
Aged widow of deep devotion, who spent all her time in the temple. A great role for an older member of the congregation. (Played by the same actor as Elizabeth, with a small costume element, such as a head scarf, to indicate the change.)

EXPANDING THE CAST

The list above requires a minimum of sixteen people, though more angels, shepherds, or wise men could be added. If you want to include a larger number of people, here are some options. (Stage directions mentioning these roles will be found in the script.)

SHEEP
Any number of children could be costumed as sheep for the shepherds to keep watch over by night.

ZECHARIAH AND SIMEON
Could be played by different actors, Zechariah remaining seated and Simeon entering from offstage.

ELIZABETH AND ANNA
Could be played by different actors, Elizabeth remaining seated and Anna entering from offstage

DONKEY AND CAMEL
Mary and Joseph could be accompanied by a donkey, and the Wise Men could be accompanied by a camel.

CHORUS
Still more people could be included by putting the lines designated for "ALL" into a group, large or small, designated as a CHORUS as may be familiar from ancient Greek theatre.

CHRISTMAS PLAY

SETTING

This play is designed to be produced in a church sanctuary, with the chancel as the stage. If the pulpit (or lectern) is moveable, it should be placed at stage right. If the pulpit is center and immovable, the action should take place in front of it.

The narrator will stand at the pulpit throughout.

Upstage, along the back of the chancel are six chairs. Five are spaced evenly from stage right through left of center. The sixth is stage left, separated to a noticeable degree, as if a gap had been left for an additional chair. In the case of a central fixed pulpit, adapt as necessary; place the chairs in front of it, or place three on each side. Four of those sitting on the chairs need to move easily to and from other parts of the stage.

The chair at the end, stage left, is for Herod, and should be visibly different from the others. It should look as much like a throne as possible; an old-fashioned preacher's chair would work nicely. The remaining chairs or stools should be ordinary (though they could be taller, like bar stools) and should match each other if possible.

At the opening "curtain" the occupants of the chairs are, script in hand, from stage right to stage left, Law and Prophets, Gabriel, Mary, Elizabeth, Zechariah and, at a distance, Herod.

Downstage of the row of chairs are several distinct places for action. Stage right is Bethlehem, marked by the presence of a manger throughout; centerstage and stage left (marked by a chair) become various locations. Upstage left, where Herod sits enthroned, is Herod's court.

Gary Neal Hansen

TIME

The narrative incorporates all the biblical passages that deal with the coming of Christ in the flesh in the first chapters of Luke, Matthew, and John.

John 1 provides the theological frame for the story in the opening and closing speeches. So technically the time spans back to "the beginning" before creation and continues to the present day because Jesus "dwelt among *us*." Both ends of that time line are crucial to the significance of Christ's coming.

The action proper begins with the promise of the conception of John the Baptist, five months before the conception of Jesus. It includes the familiar core stories of Jesus' birth and then continues all the way through the flight to Egypt and return.

This means that, unlike most Christmas pageants, *Christmas Play* includes the very dark event of Herod's "slaughter of the innocents." This is what makes vivid sense of John's declaration that, in Christ, light has come into the real world and that darkness has not overcome it. Without this it would be just a sweet story rather than the drama of salvation.

These biblical texts are woven into one harmonious narrative without formal division into scenes. Harmonization mutes the real differences between the versions of the story, but it also reflects the way Christians have remembered these stories down through the centuries.

NOTES ON THE TEXT AND STYLE OF PRODUCTION

All spoken text is from the English Standard Version, a recent translation that builds on the heritage of the Authorized or King James Version of the Bible. The ESV preserves much of the poetry of the KJV but removes all archaic language other than an occasional use of "man" or "men" where many would prefer something like "humanity."

The biblical text is used in a modified Reader's Theatre fashion. In Reader's Theatre the actors sit and read from the script rather than memorizing and acting it out. When Scripture attributes a speech to someone, that character will read that speech. At times indirect speech, or simple description associated with a person, will be read by that character as well. Also, in particular in the opening and closing segments from John, long segments that could have been tedious if spoken by the narrator have been divided up and put in the mouths of characters whose later or earlier action connects with the words.

In *Christmas Play*, the Reader's Theatre format is really a frame for a semi-staged production, including the elements of the traditional children's Christmas pageant. Mary, Gabriel, Zechariah/Simeon and Elizabeth/Anna begin on chairs as in Reader's Theatre, but leave them to join the action as needed. Other characters enter and exit as needed.

The production can be intergenerational, or can be fully cast with youth and children. Children can play simple parts (angels, wise men, shepherds and sheep), and adults or youth can play those with more speeches, including all those seated on the chairs. Perhaps the only part where age matters is Mary, who should be played by a young person.

As discussed in the cast list, the size of the cast can be expanded if a church has a large group of children or adults who want to take part.

It would also be possible to use the script for a straightforward Reader's Theater, by adding chairs for all the speaking parts and eliminating all stage action.

NOTES TO DIRECTORS AND ACTORS

1. The single most important instruction to all participants is to not allow any pauses between lines. Exceptions to this should be few and intentional. If even a beat of silence happens between every line, the whole production will drag. This is especially the case when the narrator's words feed directly into a character's line. Picking up cues in this way can be rehearsed in a read-through with each actor beginning to speak while the last word of the previous actor's line is being spoken.

2. The action needs to happen during, not after, the relevant speeches. If speeches and action are not simultaneous, the performance will drag. I have tried to place stage directions directly above the lines which should be spoken as the action happens.

3. When lines are assigned to "all" (or to a chorus), directors should rehearse diligently for unison and clarity. If these words are not spoken precisely in unison, the audience may well not understand them at all.

4. Lines in square brackets may be cut if so desired. The script includes the full ESV text of the biblical passages, but on several occasions brief transitional words ("he said" "she said") are not needed because the text is being spoken. The director should feel free to cut these lines if it improves the production.

5. On a few occasions the ESV uses "man" or "men" to refer to humanity in general. Many Christians today find gender-neutral language communicates more clearly in such cases. Directors may wish to consult the NRSV or NIV to find alternate wording for these lines.

CHRISTMAS PLAY

[JOHN 1:1-8]

(At the opening "curtain" the Narrator is at the pulpit and, from upstage right to upstage left, the following characters are seated in chairs, script in hand: Law and Prophets, Gabriel, Mary, Elizabeth, Zechariah, and at a distance, Herod. Down right is a manger. Down left is a chair.)

NARRATOR
In the beginning was the Word, and the Word was with God, and the Word was God. He was in the beginning with God. All things were made through him, and without him was not any thing made that was made.

MARY
In him was life, and the life was the light of men.

HEROD
(Sits forward, elbows on knees.)
The light shines in the darkness, and the darkness has not overcome it.

ZECHARIAH
There was a man sent from God, whose name was John. He came as a witness, to bear witness about the light, that all might believe through him. He was not the light, but came to bear witness about the light.

[LUKE 1]

NARRATOR
Inasmuch as many have undertaken to compile a narrative of the things that have been accomplished among us,

ALL (or CHORUS)
just as those who from the beginning were eyewitnesses and ministers of the word have delivered them to us,

NARRATOR
it seemed good to me also, having followed all things closely for some time past, to write an orderly account for you, most excellent Theophilus, that you may have certainty concerning the things you have been taught.

ZECHARIAH
(Rises)
In the days of Herod, king of Judea, there was a priest named Zechariah, of the division of Abijah.

ELIZABETH
(Raises hand)
And he had a wife from the daughters of Aaron, and her name was Elizabeth.

NARRATOR
And they were both righteous before God, walking blamelessly in all the commandments and statutes of the Lord. But they had no child, because Elizabeth was barren, and both were advanced in years.

ZECHARIAH
(Crosses downstage)
Now while he was serving as priest before God when his division

ZECHARIAH (CONT'D)
was on duty, according to the custom of the priesthood, he was chosen by lot to enter the temple of the Lord and burn incense.

ALL except Zechariah (or CHORUS)
And the whole multitude of the people were praying outside at the hour of incense.

NARRATOR
And there appeared to him an angel of the Lord standing on the right side of the altar of incense. And Zechariah was troubled when he saw him, and fear fell upon him. But the angel said to him,

GABRIEL
Do not be afraid, Zechariah, for your prayer has been heard, and your wife Elizabeth will bear you a son, and you shall call his name John. And you will have joy and gladness, and many will rejoice at his birth, for he will be great before the Lord. And he must not drink wine or strong drink, and he will be filled with the Holy Spirit, even from his mother's womb. And he will turn many of the children of Israel to the Lord their God, and he will go before him in the spirit and power of Elijah, to turn the hearts of the fathers to the children, and the disobedient to the wisdom of the just, to make ready for the Lord a people prepared.

[NARRATOR]
[And Zechariah said to the angel,]

ZECHARIAH
How shall I know this? For I am an old man, and my wife is advanced in years.

[NARRATOR]
[And the angel answered him,]

GABRIEL

(Gabriel rises, crosses to Zechariah)
I am Gabriel. I stand in the presence of God, and I was sent to speak to you and to bring you this good news. And behold, you will be silent and unable to speak until the day that these things take place, because you did not believe my words, which will be fulfilled in their time.
(Returns to seat)

NARRATOR

And the people were waiting for Zechariah, and they were wondering at his delay in the temple. And when he came out, he was unable to speak to them, and they realized that he had seen a vision in the temple. And he kept making signs to them and remained mute.
(Zechariah returns to seat, making signs to the others.)
And when his time of service was ended, he went to his home. After these days his wife Elizabeth conceived, and for five months she kept herself hidden, saying,

ELIZABETH

Thus the Lord has done for me in the days when he looked on me, to take away my reproach among people.

NARRATOR

In the sixth month the angel Gabriel was sent from God to a city of Galilee named Nazareth, to a virgin betrothed to a man whose name was Joseph, of the house of David. And the virgin's name was Mary. And he came to her and said,

GABRIEL

Greetings, O favored one, the Lord is with you!

MARY

But she was greatly troubled at the saying, and tried to discern what sort of greeting this might be.

CHRISTMAS PLAY

GABRIEL

And the angel said to her, Do not be afraid, Mary, for you have found favor with God. And behold, you will conceive in your womb and bear a son, and you shall call his name Jesus. He will be great and will be called the Son of the Most High. And the Lord God will give to him the throne of his father David, and he will reign over the house of Jacob forever, and of his kingdom there will be no end.

[NARRATOR]

[And Mary said to the angel,]

MARY

How will this be, since I am a virgin?

[NARRATOR]

[And the angel answered and said unto her,]

GABRIEL

(Stands)

The Holy Spirit will come upon you, and the power of the Most High will overshadow you; therefore the child to be born will be called holy—the Son of God. And behold, your relative Elizabeth in her old age has also conceived a son, and this is the sixth month with her who was called barren. For nothing will be impossible with God.

[NARRATOR]

[And Mary said,]

MARY

(Kneels)

Behold, I am the servant of the Lord; let it be to me according to your word.

NARRATOR

(Gabriel sits. Elizabeth crosses down left, sits on chair.)
And the angel departed from her.
(Mary crosses to join Elizabeth.)
In those days Mary arose and went with haste into the hill country, to a town in Judah, and she entered the house of Zechariah and greeted Elizabeth.
(Rises to greet her. They hug; Elizabeth steps back.)
And when Elizabeth heard the greeting of Mary, the baby leaped in her womb. And Elizabeth was filled with the Holy Spirit, and she exclaimed with a loud cry,

ELIZABETH

Blessed are you among women, and blessed is the fruit of your womb! And why is this granted to me that the mother of my Lord should come to me? For behold, when the sound of your greeting came to my ears, the baby in my womb leaped for joy. And blessed is she who believed that there would be a fulfillment of what was spoken to her from the Lord.

[NARRATOR]

[And Mary said,]

MARY

My soul magnifies the Lord, and my spirit rejoices in God my Savior,
for he has looked on the humble estate of his servant.
For behold, from now on all generations will call me blessed;
for he who is mighty has done great things for me, and holy is his name.
And his mercy is for those who fear him from generation to generation.
He has shown strength with his arm;
he has scattered the proud in the thoughts of their hearts;
he has brought down the mighty from their thrones and exalted

MARY (CONT'D)

those of humble estate;
he has filled the hungry with good things, and the rich he has sent away empty.
He has helped his servant Israel, in remembrance of his mercy, as he spoke to our fathers, to Abraham and to his offspring forever.

NARRATOR

(Mary returns to her seat. Zechariah joins Elizabeth. She picks up a doll, the baby John the Baptist, from a hidden location, possibly from the folds of her robe, joyfully cradling him in her arms.)

And Mary remained with her about three months and returned to her home. Now the time came for Elizabeth to give birth, and she bore a son. And her neighbors and relatives heard that the Lord had shown great mercy to her, and they rejoiced with her. And on the eighth day they came to circumcise the child. And they would have called him

ALL except Zechariah and Elizabeth, (or CHORUS)

Zechariah

NARRATOR

after his father, but his mother answered,

ELIZABETH

No; he shall be called John.

NARRATOR

And they said to her,

ALL except Zechariah and Elizabeth (or CHORUS)
None of your relatives is called by this name.

NARRATOR
(ALL except Elizabeth [or CHORUS] "sign" to Zechariah in unison, "You call him what?" 1. Point to Zechariah 2. Open and close hand as if talking. 3. Point to John. 4. Hold up hands and shoulders in a questioning shrug.)

And they made signs to his father, inquiring what he wanted him to be called.

(Zechariah gestures writing; someone hands him a pad and pen)

And he asked for a writing tablet and wrote,

(Looks down at Zechariah, as Zechariah writes each word)

His
name
is
John.

And they all wondered.

ZECHARIAH
And immediately his mouth was opened and his tongue loosed, and he spoke, blessing God.

NARRATOR
And fear came on all their neighbors. And all these things were talked about through all the hill country of Judea, and all who heard them laid them up in their hearts, saying,

ALL except Zechariah (or CHORUS)
What then will this child be?

NARRATOR
(Zechariah holds baby John)

For the hand of the Lord was with him. And his father Zechariah was filled with the Holy Spirit and prophesied, saying,

Christmas Play

ZECHARIAH

Blessed be the Lord God of Israel,
for he has visited and redeemed his people
and has raised up a horn of salvation for us
in the house of his servant David,
as he spoke by the mouth of his holy prophets from of old,
that we should be saved from our enemies
and from the hand of all who hate us;
to show the mercy promised to our fathers
and to remember his holy covenant,
the oath that he swore to our father Abraham,
to grant us that we, being delivered from the hand of our enemies,
might serve him without fear,
in holiness and righteousness before him all our days.
And you, child, will be called the prophet of the Most High;
for you will go before the Lord to prepare his ways,
to give knowledge of salvation to his people in the forgiveness of their sins,
because of the tender mercy of our God,
whereby the sunrise shall visit us from on high
to give light to those who sit in darkness
and in the shadow of death,
to guide our feet into the way of peace.
  (Zechariah and Elizabeth return to chairs)

NARRATOR

And the child grew and became strong in spirit, and he was in the wilderness until the day of his public appearance to Israel.

[MATTHEW 1:18-25]

NARRATOR

Now the birth of Jesus Christ took place in this way. When his mother Mary had been betrothed to Joseph, before they came together she was found to be with child from the Holy Spirit.

JOSEPH

(Joseph enters stage right, crosses to down center)
And her husband Joseph, being a just man and unwilling to put her to shame, resolved to divorce her quietly.

NARRATOR

(Joseph lays down.)
But as he considered these things, behold, an angel of the Lord appeared to him in a dream, saying,

GABRIEL

(Joseph sits up)
Joseph, son of David, do not fear to take Mary as your wife, for that which is conceived in her is from the Holy Spirit. She will bear a son, and you shall call his name Jesus, for he will save his people from their sins.

NARRATOR

All this took place to fulfill what the Lord had spoken by the prophet:

LAW AND PROPHETS

(Stands to read from scroll)
"Behold, the virgin shall conceive and bear a son, and they shall call his name Immanuel" (which means, God with us).
(Sits)

Christmas Play

JOSEPH
(Joseph rises, crosses to Mary, and put his arm around her shoulder.)
When Joseph woke from sleep, he did as the angel of the Lord commanded him: he took his wife, but knew her not until she had given birth to a son. And he called his name Jesus.

Gary Neal Hansen

[LUKE 2:1-20]

NARRATOR
(Mary and Joseph exit right.)
In those days a decree went out from Caesar Augustus that all the world should be registered. This was the first registration when Quirinius was governor of Syria. And all went to be registered, each to his own town.

JOSEPH
(Joseph and Mary enter, with a Donkey if casting permits, up an aisle from the back of the sanctuary. They proceed to down center. Innkeeper enters stage left, and sits in the chair behind an imaginary door. Joseph, Mary, and Donkey cross down left to the Innkeeper's door during these two lines, and knock.)
And Joseph also went up from Galilee, from the town of Nazareth, to Judea, to the city of David, which is called Bethlehem, because he was of the house and lineage of David,

MARY
(She is uncomfortably pregnant.)
to be registered with Mary, his betrothed, who was with child.
(Innkeeper rises and opens the door. Silently Joseph asks for a room for his pregnant wife. Innkeeper shakes head, and points to the manger, stage right. They cross right, behind the manger. Joseph helps Mary to her knees)

NARRATOR
And while they were there, the time came for her to give birth.
(Mary picks up a doll, the Baby Jesus, from a hidden place, possibly the folds of her robe, wraps cloths around him, and places him in the manger. Both kneel, gazing at the child with folded hands. A star should rise over the manger, or at least somewhere stage right.)

Christmas Play

NARRATOR (CONT'D)
And she gave birth to her firstborn son and wrapped him in swaddling cloths and laid him in a manger,

INNKEEPER
because there was no place for them in the inn.
(Innkeeper closes the door and exits stage left.)

NARRATOR
(Shepherds enter stage left, with Sheep if casting permits, and sit.)
And in the same region there were shepherds out in the field, keeping watch over their flock by night.
(Gabriel crosses to stage left, behind the shepherds. Shepherds show fear.)
And an angel of the Lord appeared to them, and the glory of the Lord shone around them,

SHEPHERDS
and they were filled with great fear.

[NARRATOR]
[And the angel said to them,]

GABRIEL
Fear not, for behold, I bring you good news of great joy that will be for all the people. For unto you is born this day in the city of David a Savior, who is Christ the Lord. And this will be a sign for you: you will find a baby wrapped in swaddling cloths and lying in a manger.
(More angels enter, above Gabriel if the church has an organ loft, or from left and flanking Gabriel)

NARRATOR
And suddenly there was with the angel a multitude of the heavenly host praising God and saying,

ALL ANGELS
(Raising hands and dancing in unison. If there is a choir to back the angels this line could be sung using "Glory to God" from Handel's "Messiah.")
Glory to God in the highest, and on earth peace among those with whom he is pleased!

NARRATOR
(Angels exit dancing to the place from which they entered.)
When the angels went away from them into heaven, the shepherds said to one another,

SHEPHERDS
Let us go over to Bethlehem and see this thing that has happened, which the Lord has made known to us.

NARRATOR
(Shepherds cross right, kneel in a semicircle before the manger, backs to audience.)
And they went with haste and found Mary and Joseph, and the baby lying in a manger.
(Shepherds get up, and scatter joyfully down all the aisles, stopping to whisper "Unto you is born this day in the city of David a Savior, who is Christ the Lord!" to individuals in the congregation as they go.)
And when they saw it, they made known the saying that had been told them concerning this child. And all who heard it wondered at what the shepherds told them.

CHRISTMAS PLAY

MARY
(Mary picks up the baby Jesus and stands with him, adoring him.)
But Mary treasured up all these things, pondering them in her heart.

SHEPHERDS
(Shepherds come back to their sheep from the places they've gone, then exit, stage left.)
And the shepherds returned, glorifying and praising God for all they had heard and seen, as it had been told them.

Gary Neal Hansen

[MATTHEW 2:1-12]

NARRATOR
(Wise Men enter in stately fashion, with a camel if casting permits, up the center aisle, and approach Herod's throne.)
Now after Jesus was born in Bethlehem of Judea in the days of Herod the king, behold, wise men from the east came to Jerusalem, saying,

WISE MEN
Where is he who has been born king of the Jews? For we saw his star when it rose and have come to worship him.

NARRATOR
When Herod the king heard this, he was troubled, and all Jerusalem with him; and assembling all the chief priests and scribes of the people, he inquired of them where the Christ was to be born. They told him,

ALL except Herod (or CHORUS)
In Bethlehem of Judea, for so it is written by the prophet:

LAW AND PROPHETS
(Standing to read from scroll)
"And you, O Bethlehem, in the land of Judah, are by no means least among the rulers of Judah; for from you shall come a ruler who will shepherd my people Israel."
(Sits)

HEROD
Then Herod summoned the wise men secretly and ascertained from them what time the star had appeared. And he sent them to Bethlehem, saying,
Go and search diligently for the child, and when you have found him, bring me word, that I too may come and

HEROD (CONT'D)
(Pause for one heartbeat)
worship him.

NARRATOR
(The Wise Men cross, in stately fashion, to Mary, Joseph, and the baby Jesus.)
After listening to the king, they went on their way. And behold, the star that they had seen when it rose went before them until it came to rest over the place where the child was. When they saw the star, they rejoiced exceedingly with great joy.
(They kneel, touching their foreheads to the ground.)
And going into the house they saw the child with Mary his mother, and they fell down and worshiped him.

WISE MAN ONE
(They offer their gifts.)
Then, opening their treasures, they offered him gifts,

WISE MAN TWO
gold and frankincense and myrrh.

WISE MAN THREE
(They rise and exit, stage right)
And being warned in a dream not to return to Herod, they departed to their own country by another way.

Gary Neal Hansen

[LUKE 2:21-38]

NARRATOR
And at the end of eight days, when he was circumcised, he was called Jesus, the name given by the angel before he was conceived in the womb.
(Mary picks up the Baby Jesus and goes with Joseph very slowly toward center stage, which is now the temple)
And when the time came for their purification according to the Law of Moses, they brought him up to Jerusalem to present him to the Lord (as it is written in the Law of the Lord,

LAW AND PROPHETS
(Standing to read from scroll.)
"Every male who first opens the womb shall be called holy to the Lord")

NARRATOR
and to offer a sacrifice according to what is said in the Law of the Lord,

LAW AND PROPHETS
(Still standing, reading from a new place in the scroll.)
"a pair of turtledoves, or two young pigeons."
(Sits.)

NARRATOR
(Simeon, having put on a headdress, stands [or, if cast separately from Zechariah, enters stage left] and crosses to center, arriving before the Holy Family. Anna, having put on a head scarf crosses down left [or if cast separately from Elizabeth, enters left] and sits on the chair.)
Now there was a man in Jerusalem, whose name was Simeon, and this man was righteous and devout, waiting for the consolation of Israel, and the Holy Spirit was upon him.

Christmas Play

SIMEON

And it had been revealed to him by the Holy Spirit that he would not see death before he had seen the Lord's Christ.

NARRATOR

(Simeon reaches out toward Mary and Joseph in greeting, as they approach.)
And he came in the Spirit into the temple,
(Simeon takes the baby Jesus in his arms, looks to heaven.)
and when the parents brought in the child Jesus, to do for him according to the custom of the Law, he took him up in his arms and blessed God and said,

SIMEON

Lord, now you are letting your servant depart in peace, according to your word; for my eyes have seen your salvation that you have prepared in the presence of all peoples, a light for revelation to the Gentiles, and for glory to your people Israel.

NARRATOR

And his father and his mother marveled at what was said about him.
(Makes the sign of the cross before them.)
And Simeon blessed them and said to Mary his mother,

SIMEON

Behold, this child is appointed for the fall and rising of many in Israel, and for a sign that is opposed (and a sword will pierce through your own soul also), so that thoughts from many hearts may be revealed.
(Simeon gives the Baby Jesus back to Mary, and returns to his seat [or exits stage left if cast separately from Zechariah]. Anna, stands and crosses to the holy family in the temple.)

NARRATOR

And there was a prophetess, Anna, the daughter of Phanuel, of the tribe of Asher.

ANNA

She was advanced in years, having lived with her husband seven years from when she was a virgin, and then as a widow until she was eighty-four. She did not depart from the temple, worshiping with fasting and prayer night and day.

(She takes the Baby Jesus in her arms and adores him, then looks joyfully to heaven.)

And coming up at that very hour she began to give thanks to God

NARRATOR

(Anna gives the baby Jesus back, and exits down the left aisle, stopping excitedly to speak with members of the congregation: "I have seen the Christ child!")

and to speak of him to all who were waiting for the redemption of Jerusalem.

(Mary, Joseph, and Baby Jesus return to the manger, stage right, and lay down to sleep.)

Christmas Play

[MATTHEW 2:13-20]

NARRATOR
(Gabriel crosses to the manger and reaches down to touch Joseph's shoulder; Joseph sits up.)
Now when they had departed, behold, an angel of the Lord appeared to Joseph in a dream and said,

GABRIEL
Rise, take the child and his mother, and flee to Egypt, and remain there until I tell you, for Herod is about to search for the child, to destroy him.

JOSEPH
(Joseph stands, reaches out to Mary. She picks up Baby Jesus, takes Joseph's hand. They exit, with donkey if there is one, stage right. Gabriel returns to seat.)
And he rose and took the child and his mother by night and departed to Egypt and remained there until the death of Herod.

NARRATOR
This was to fulfill what the Lord had spoken by the prophet,

LAW AND PROPHETS
(Standing to read from scroll.)
"Out of Egypt I called my son."
(Sits)

HEROD
(Rises. Note that the text says he was "furious." Or, as the KJV put it, he was "exceeding wroth.")
Then Herod, when he saw that he had been tricked by the wise men, became furious, and he sent and killed all the male children in Bethlehem and in all that region who were two years old or under,

according to the time that he had ascertained from the wise men.
(Sits)

NARRATOR
(Pause one heartbeat. Soberly.)
Then was fulfilled what was spoken by the prophet Jeremiah:

LAW AND PROPHETS
(Sits, head bowed, reads slowly from scroll.)
"A voice was heard in Ramah, weeping and loud lamentation, Rachel weeping for her children; she refused to be comforted, because they are no more."
(Hanging head, drops scroll.)

NARRATOR
(Gabriel stands. Joseph appears from stage right where he has exited; he stays just at the edge of the stage and looks at Gabriel.)
But when Herod died, behold, an angel of the Lord appeared in a dream to Joseph in Egypt, saying

GABRIEL
Rise, take the child and his mother, and go to the land of Israel, for those who sought the child's life are dead.
(Gabriel sits.)

CHRISTMAS PLAY

[LUKE 2:39-40]

NARRATOR
(Mary, Joseph, and Donkey, with Baby Jesus, enter and come down center, which is now Nazareth. They sit or kneel, center, and silently play with the Baby Jesus, enjoying him.)
And when they had performed everything according to the Law of the Lord, they returned into Galilee, to their own town of Nazareth. And the child grew and became strong, filled with wisdom. And the favor of God was upon him.

Gary Neal Hansen

[JOHN 1:9-14]

(All other cast members enter, span the stage behind the holy family and in front of the chairs, in their groups: Shepherds, Angels, Wise Men, Innkeeper, Simeon and Anna.)

NARRATOR
(When all are in place)
The true light, which gives light to everyone, was coming into the world.

HEROD
(Rises, steps forward one step.)
He was in the world, and the world was made through him, yet the world did not know him.

INNKEEPER
(Step forward one step.)
He came to his own, and his own people did not receive him.

SHEPHERDS, WISE MEN, SIMEON, ANNA
(All step forward one step.)
But to all who did receive him, who believed in his name, he gave the right to become children of God,

JOSEPH
(Rising, with Mary.)
who were born, not of blood nor of the will of the flesh nor of the will of man, but of God.

ALL (Standing. If using a CHORUS, this line includes them and all other cast members.)
And the Word became flesh and dwelt among us, and we have

ALL (CONT'D)
seen his glory, glory as of the only Son from the Father, full of grace and truth.

(Blackout)

www.ingramcontent.com/pod-product-compliance
Lightning Source LLC
Chambersburg PA
CBHW020628300426
44112CB00010B/1248